A Really Basic Introduction to

Capital Gains Tax

By Michael A Lambarth

Michael Lambarth

Text copyright (c) 2015

Michael A Lambarth

All Rights Reserved

A Really Basic Introduction to Capital Gains Tax

Table of Contents

Chapter 1 – Introduction 4

Chapter 2 – What is Capital Gains Tax? 7

Chapter 3 – A basic calculation 15

Chapter 4 – The rates of tax 19

Chapter 5 – Selling part of an asset 22

Chapter 6 – Chattels 27

Chapter 7 – Shares 32

Chapter 8 – Tax reliefs 39

Chapter 9 – Losses 52

Chapter 10 – Companies 56

Chapter 1 – Introduction

Welcome to "A Really Basic Introduction to Capital Gains Tax". Have you ever tried to find introductory books about complicated topics, only to be completely lost after a few pages? Usually, the author starts the book by explaining how basic the book will be, and then appears to forget this altogether on the very next page when he or she starts to use words which you do not understand. Having stated that no previous knowledge is required, they very quickly start to assume that you know the meaning of specific terms, or they say that it would be helpful to know a bit about some other subject before reading the book. The fact that you have purchased a book which was described as a basic introduction to the subject seems to evade them completely.

This book is exactly what it says it is; a really basic introduction to UK capital gains tax. No previous knowledge of the tax system is needed. I will explain all terms in full as we go along and will not try to impress you with my knowledge of complex terminology. This book will give you a good understanding of capital gains tax and how it works. It will help you understand your own personal tax affairs. It will also help you if you are undertaking any course of study where knowledge of capital gains tax is required, such as law, accounting, business, management or finance. Needless to say, an introductory book of this nature does have its limitations. After reading through it, you will not be able to give detailed tax advice to other people. Nor will you understand the subject in depth, or be able to talk to a professional adviser on their own terms. It is, after all, a really basic introduction to the topic.

So who am I to think that I can write such a book? Well, I have respected tax qualifications, and I am a qualified higher education teacher and a qualified solicitor. Hopefully I therefore have the skills needed to convey this subject in a clear and concise manner. I have spent many hours explaining the principles in this book to students, colleagues and clients, so I am convinced you will be able to follow what I am saying.

I have tried to keep this book as short as possible, so that it is manageable, and so that you don't lose interest or feel intimidated after just a couple of chapters. The other thing I have done is to try to keep things real and practical. Tax is a difficult enough subject to grasp, without trying to do so in the abstract. The book contains examples which show how things work, and build on each other to introduce new ideas. This means that your understanding is automatically consolidated as you read and that you should be able to read this book from start to finish and end up with a pretty good understanding of what is going on. You shouldn't have to keep flicking back to previous sections to remind yourself of what you read yesterday, or last week. By reading the same ideas again and again, in different contexts, I hope that you will end up with a confident, basic understanding of the subject.

The facts and figures are correct as at October 2015, but should remain valid for the current tax year (until 5th April 2016). Many of the principles are likely to remain relevant for some time after that, but that is outside of my control.

I hope you enjoy the book.

Chapter 2 – What is Capital Gains Tax?

We should probably start with a quick word about taxation generally. Taxation is basically the money the government collects in order to run the country. It collects many different types of tax, one of which is capital gains tax. The tax is paid to the government, which then uses it to pay for hospitals, new roads, schools and so on. That all sounds nice and simple but is, of course, actually incredibly complex. Billions of pounds are raised through taxation and the decisions made about how to spend that money are largely political. Even the decision as to how much tax to charge is a political "hot potato". Lowering the rate at which the main taxes are charged has often been seen as a major vote winner in political circles.

Capital gains tax is not a tax that will affect everyone. In fact, most people will go through their entire lives without ever paying a penny in capital gains tax. It is not a tax which raises a huge amount of money for the government when compared to other taxes such as income tax or value added tax. However, when it does become payable it can give rise to a significant amount of tax for the individual taxpayer.

As with most taxes, the name "capital gains tax" is useful to keep in mind when thinking about the circumstances in which the tax might be relevant. Let's work through the name and have a think about what it tells us. Obviously the word "tax" tells us this is a tax. But what about "capital" and "gains"? What do they mean?

"Capital" is something of a technical term when it comes to finance and taxation. It can in fact have different meanings depending on the circumstances. It does however have a particular meaning in the context of capital gains tax. Perhaps the best starting point for explaining what is meant by capital is to say that anything which is of an income nature cannot therefore be "capital". This means we now need to think about what we mean by "income". Stay with me, it will become clearer!

For taxation purposes, the definition of "income" is very complicated and there have been many legal court cases where the parties have argued over the meaning of the word in different situations. For our purposes, it is probably sufficient to think about the main things which would fall into this category. One thing to remember about income though, is that it is usually a recurring payment of some kind; in other words, something which is received again and again. Income includes money earned from employment (wages and salaries), money received on investments such as interest on bank savings, and income from a business or trade. Hopefully you can see that these types of receipts are things which recur. Wages and salaries are received every week or every month. Interest is usually paid every month or every year. Income is received from a business every time it makes a sale.

So those things are income and therefore not capital. Income receipts are subject to income tax (see "A Really Basic Introduction to Income Tax" for more details). They are not subject to capital gains tax. "Capital" therefore means "not income" or "not recurring" to some extent. We could say that capital gains tax applies generally to one-off events rather than recurring events.

Let's consider Adam, who is a landlord. He owns several houses which he rents out to students studying at the local university. The monthly rent from all the houses adds up to £4,000. This money is something which Adam receives on a recurring basis (monthly) and it is a receipt from his property letting business. It is therefore classed as income and Adam will pay income tax on the £48,000 that he receives from this business in the year (£4,000 multiplied by 12 months). If Adam continues to run his business in this way then he will be subject only to income tax on the rent; capital gains tax will not be an issue for him.

However, if Adam decides to sell one of his houses, then capital gains tax might well become relevant. Adam's houses are, for his business, "capital items". This means they were purchased not with a view to selling them on for a profit (as a property developer might do) but to retain and be utilised within his business. His business or trade consists of renting houses to students, not buying and selling houses for profit. Therefore, if Adam does decide to sell one of his houses, perhaps because it does not tend to let as readily as his other houses, then this would be a one-off transaction, or a capital transaction. The proceeds would not be subject to income tax, but potentially to capital gains tax.

For another example, think of a high street store, perhaps one that sells shoes. The sale of shoes would be the trade in which this shop has decided to conduct business. Any shoe sales (and related products) would therefore give rise to a receipt of income. This would be subject to income tax in the hands of the business owner (assuming that it is not run by a company, which have different rules which we will cover briefly later in the book). If, however, the business sold one of its shops, then this would be a capital transaction - a one-off deal which is not generally within the trade of selling shoes. This property sale would be a capital transaction and potentially subject to capital gains tax.

Let's look at one final example. Basil works as a lecturer in a university. He has a general interest in works of art and owns several quite valuable paintings which are on display in his house. To make room for his latest purchase, he decides to sell one from his existing collection. Basil will pay income tax on his salary received from the university, but the sale of the painting will be a capital transaction for him. He is not an art dealer, so the money received from a one-off sale of a painting will not be classed as income. The proceeds may, however, leave him facing a capital gains tax charge. If Basil began to buy and sell works of art on a regular basis, then he may well be classed as a self-employed art dealer and in that case, the money received from the sale of his paintings would be classed as income and subject to income tax.

Where we have referred to "one-off" transactions above, we don't literally mean just one. If Basil sells the odd painting every couple of years, then he is unlikely to be classed as an art dealer. If he does it several times a month then he might well be classed as an art dealer. It very much depends on the regularity of the event and the nature of the thing that is being traded or supplied.

So now that we have an idea of what we mean by "capital", we can move on to look at the other word in the name of this tax, "gains".

We don't need to make this more complicated than it needs to be. I make a gain where I sell something for more than I bought it for. I therefore make a capital gain where I sell something which is "capital" in nature (in the way that we have just been talking about above) for more than I bought it for. For example, if I buy a painting (assuming I am not an art dealer) for £5,000 and sell it for £12,000, then I have made a gain of £7,000. It is this gain on which I will potentially be charged to capital gains tax. Note that the tax only arises when I dispose of the painting. A sale is the most common method of disposing of something, but I might also have to pay capital gains tax if, for example, I give something away or if it is destroyed and I receive insurance money for it. Another important point here is that capital gains tax is not generally payable on death. Even though the deceased person will effectively dispose of their assets (to those people named in their will for example) no capital gains tax is paid. Instead, the value of the assets transferred is generally subject to inheritance tax, but that is something to be covered in a different book!

You may have noticed that the examples I have used in this chapter have involved works of art and property. The reason for that choice is that I need examples of things which go up in value. As we have seen, capital gains tax is payable on gains; where something is sold for more than it was purchased for. If you stop and think about this for a moment, not many things actually go up in value – most lose their value as soon as they are purchased. The main examples of things which go up in value are property, certain types of speciality objects such as art, antiques and jewellery, and shares. By shares I mean the shares that it is possible to buy in a company which denote who owns that company. If I buy shares in Tesco, then I own a part of that company, albeit a very small part. If I am lucky, those shares should go up in value over time. When I sell them I will make a gain, and that gain may well be charged to capital gains tax.

Finally for this chapter, it is important to have a quick word about tax years. Unfortunately, when it comes to capital gains tax (and many other taxes), when we talk in terms of a year we are not talking about 1st January to 31st December as we might immediately think. The "tax year" runs from 6th April in one year up until 5th April in the next year (for historical, if somewhat uncertain, reasons). When we need to calculate a person's gains for the tax year, we therefore need to look for disposals of assets that took place between 6th April in one year and 5th April in the next.

I hope that this chapter has given you a good understanding of what capital gains tax is and when it might become payable. The following chapters will cover example scenarios with full explanations to help you appreciate some of the more detailed rules that apply and how the tax calculations work.

Chapter 3 – A basic calculation

Let's start with a basic capital gains tax calculation. Carole owns a holiday cottage on the coast which she has used for weekend getaways for the last ten years or so. She bought it for £150,000, and is now selling it for £210,000. We can see from those figures that the basic gain made by Carole is £60,000. This figure is found by starting with the amount she sold it for (£210,000) and subtracting the amount she paid for it in the first place (£150,000). In other words, the value of the cottage has increased by £60,000 during her period of ownership.

However, Carole is allowed to deduct certain expenditure which she has incurred on the cottage. Firstly, she can deduct her expenses incurred in buying and selling the cottage. These can include legal fees and estate agent fees for example. By deducting these costs, she is thereby reducing her gain and therefore reducing the amount of tax that she needs to pay. The other main type of expenditure she can deduct is the cost of any improvements that she has made to the property which are reflected in the value of the cottage. This won't include maintenance such as repairs or decoration, but would include the building of an extension for example.

Let's assume that Carole's costs incurred on the sale and the purchase totalled £8,000, and that she built an extension to the cottage a few years ago which cost £15,000. The total of these costs is therefore £23,000, and this can be deducted from her gain of £60,000 to give a revised gain of £37,000. This will have the effect of reducing her capital gains tax bill considerably.

The other thing that is available to reduce her gain is her annual allowance. All individuals receive an allowance of £11,100 for each tax year. Remember, a tax year runs from 6th April in one year to 5th April in the next year. Any capital gains I make in any tax year which total less than the annual allowance will not therefore attract any capital gains tax. The allowance tends to increase a little each year, something which is often announced in the Budget speech made by the Chancellor of the Exchequer, usually around March each year. This annual allowance provides an opportunity for some easy and legal tax planning. If a person intends to dispose of a couple of assets in a tax year, each giving rise to a capital gain of £10,000, then by delaying the sale of one of those assets until the next tax year, both gains would fall within the annual allowance and not be subject to capital gains tax. If both *are* sold in the same tax year, then of the £20,000 gain that is made, only £11,100 would be covered by the allowance and the remaining £8,900 would be subject to tax.

Returning to Carole and the sale of her cottage, the gain she has made totals £37,000 after deduction of related costs and expenses. She can now deduct her annual allowance of £11,100 to leave a gain of £25,900. That is the gain that will be subject to capital gains tax. Before we can determine how much tax that will be, we need to look at the rates of capital gains tax, which we will do in the next chapter.

Before we go there, you might just be wondering about the sale of houses in general and how capital gains tax applies. The answer is that the sales of most residential houses are exempt from capital gains tax. This is due to a tax relief which is available on the sale of a person's main private residence. If I only own one house and it is the place where I live then, when I sell it, any gain I make will be exempt from capital gains tax. This applies to the vast majority of homeowners of course. If I do own more than one house, then only the one which is my *main* residence will attract the relief; the other properties are likely to give rise to a capital gains tax charge if they are sold for more than they were purchased for. Carole is selling a holiday cottage and the implication is that it is not her main residence, therefore she faces a capital gains tax charge on the gain resulting from the sale. The detailed rules on the private residence exemption are complex, especially where houses are occupied as a main residence for periods of time but not for other periods. For example, if houses are let out fully or in part, or are used for business purposes, or are unoccupied for periods of time, then the relief may not be available or may be restricted. For most homeowners however, the relief is a simple one which applies automatically to a person's sole or main residence, without the need to apply to HM Revenue and Customs for it to become operational.

This chapter has introduced you to the method of calculating a basic gain charged to capital gains tax. Starting with the sale proceeds, we can deduct the original purchase price and any related costs and expenses, as well as the annual allowance. The resulting figure is the amount on which tax is charged.

Chapter 4 – The rates of tax

The rates at which capital gains tax is paid give rise to some complications. On the face of it, the position seems quite straightforward; the rates of tax are 18% and 28%. The difficulty arises when we start to consider which of the two rates applies to a particular individual. The reason for the complication is that the rate at which a person pays capital gains tax depends on their *income tax* position. This book is not about income tax. However, if we are to grasp a good understanding of capital gains tax, then we do need to consider income tax for a moment.

As we discussed earlier in this book, income tax is paid on money received regularly such as wages and salaries, interest on savings and dividends received in relation to any shares that a person owns. The important point for us is that income tax is paid at different rates depending which "band" of income a person falls into. A "basic rate taxpayer" is someone who has sufficient income in a year to earn more than the income tax personal allowance (currently £10,600) and therefore pay income tax at 20% (or 10% on dividends) on the remainder of their income, but not enough to be paying tax at the higher rate of

40% (or 32.5% on dividends). The higher rate generally only applies where someone earns more than £42,385 in a tax year, and then it only applies to the income above this level. This figure tends to change a little each year.

So how does this affect the rate of capital gains tax? Well, the rule is that if you will be paying income tax at 40% on any of your income in a particular tax year, then all your capital gains that arise in the same year (after deduction of your annual allowance) will be subject to capital gains tax at the higher rate of 28%.

On the other hand, if you won't be paying any income tax at 40%, then your capital gains will be taxed at the lower rate of 18%. However, the 18% rate will only apply to gains that fall within the 20% band for income tax. Once that is "full", then the remaining gains will be taxed at 40%. Perhaps an example would help here.

We'll keep the figures easy so that it is clear what is happening. Let's assume that Carole has a total income in the current tax year of £22,385. For income tax purposes, she can deduct her income tax personal allowance of £10,600, leaving her with income of £11,785 which will be subject to income tax. She could potentially earn a further

£20,000 before she is required to pay income tax at the higher rate of 40% which, remember, kicks in at £42,385 for most taxpayers. Thinking back to her capital gain from chapter 3, she made a gain of £25,900 on the sale of her cottage. Therefore, the first £20,000 of this gain will be taxed at 18%, because it fits within the remaining basic rate income tax band which Carole has not used, and the other £5,900 will be taxed at the higher rate of 28% because by then Carole is effectively a higher rate taxpayer.

Her capital gains tax bill will therefore be 18% of £20,000, which is £3,600, plus 28% of £5,900, which is £1,652. That's a total capital gains tax bill of £5,252.

I've tried to keep this chapter brief so as not to delve into the murky depths of income tax too far. I hope it has given you enough information to understand how the rates of capital gains tax apply.

Chapter 5 – Selling part of an asset

There are special rules that apply when selling part of an asset. Most commonly, this applies to the sale of part of a piece of land. Let's consider Davina, who owns a plot of land and wants to sell a fairly small part of it. In fact, her plot of land is a large field, but there is a small corner of the field on which she has managed to obtain planning permission from the local authority to build a house. Davina doesn't want to build the house herself, but always intended to sell the land with planning permission attached so that someone else could build the house. Of course, the planning permission makes the land much more valuable than it would otherwise have been.

Davina bought the field ten years ago from a local farmer for £20,000. She keeps her horse in it. She is now offering to sell the small corner plot with planning permission for £60,000.

Thinking about her capital gains tax position, Davina will receive £60,000 when she sells the corner plot. Usually, we would then deduct the cost of the land. She paid £20,000 for the field and so this would give rise to a gain of

£40,000. However, let's just think about that for a moment. Did she really pay £20,000 for the land that she is selling? The answer is no, she did not. She paid £20,000 for the *whole* field. She is only selling a small part of it. We need to know what *proportion* of the field she is selling, so that we can work out what proportion of the original purchase price of the field related to the bit she is now selling.

When we talk about the proportion that she is now selling, we don't mean the proportion in terms of size, we mean in terms of value. It sounds like the plot of land Davina is selling is actually a very small corner of the whole field. However, in terms of value, it seems like it is pretty high compared to the rest of the field (which doesn't have planning permission of course).

In order to calculate this proportion we need to know the value of the rest of the field, excluding the corner plot that she is selling. In other words, we need the value of the land that she is retaining. Let's assume the value of that land is £40,000. What that means is that the value of the whole field is now £100,000. That's made up of the £60,000 corner plot and the £40,000 field excluding the corner plot. The value of the part she is selling is of course £60,000. She is therefore selling a proportion of the field equal to 60,000 divided by 100,000. In other words, she is selling six tenths, or 60% if you prefer, of the field.

This 60% figure is important. It tells us what proportion of historical expenditure Davina can deduct from the gain. By historical expenditure, I really mean expenditure which relates to the whole field. For example, the £20,000 purchase price that she paid relates to the whole field. We need to know what part of that expenditure we can deduct on the sale of the corner plot, and we now know that the answer is 60%. Applying this percentage to the £20,000, it gives £12,000. So £12,000 of the original purchase price relates to the corner plot and the other £8,000 relates to the rest of the field (that she is keeping).

Returning to Davina's capital gains tax calculation, we now know that she can deduct a £12,000 "purchase price" from the sale proceeds of £60,000, giving her a basic gain of £48,000. The same principle applies to other costs which relate to the whole field. For example, any costs that she incurred when she purchased the field in the first place (such as legal fees) need to be apportioned between the part she is selling and the part she is keeping. Assuming her costs were £3,000, then she can now deduct 60%, or £1,800, from her gain in respect of these costs. That will reduce her gain from £48,000 to £46,200.

Of course, the costs that she incurs on the sale of the corner plot relate *only* to the corner plot and therefore she can claim *all* of those costs. Let's assume they total £2,200. That brings her gain down from £46,200 to £44,000.

It is worth thinking about any costs Davina may have spent on improving the land. If she had, for example, spent £4,000 to put a new drainage system into the whole field then she could only claim a deduction for the part of that cost which applied to the part she is now selling (which, as we have seen, would be 60%). However, if she made improvements only to the plot she is selling in order, for example, to obtain planning permission or to make it more saleable, then she could potentially deduct the whole of that amount from her gain as it all relates to the part being sold. Finally, any improvements made *only* to parts of the field which she is not selling cannot be deducted at all in relation to the sale of the corner plot.

This chapter has looked at the situation that arises when someone sells part of an asset. This will often be land and buildings. The important point to remember is that only expenditure which relates to that part of the land being sold can be deducted from the gain.

Chapter 6 – Chattels

A "chattel" refers to moveable assets which people own such as cars, computers, books, jewellery and so on.

Many of these things are "wasting assets". A wasting asset is an asset which is not expected to have a life of more than 50 years. Wasting assets are exempt from capital gains tax. Many assets fall into this category and the vast majority of such assets lose value over time in any case, meaning that no capital gains tax would have been payable in any event. Televisions, washing machines, computers and cars fall into this category.

There are, however, some chattels which do tend to increase in value as time passes and are expected to last in excess of 50 years, so are not wasting assets. These include works of art, antiques and fine jewellery. When a chattel of this nature is sold it may well give rise to a capital gain. There are special rules which apply where the value of such items is relatively small. The rules themselves can be a little complex but are manageable if applied correctly. The rules state that no capital gains tax is payable where a chattel is sold for not more than £6,000. This is normally the amount received from the purchaser, but can be replaced with the market value where something is given away, or sold to a family member or close business associate.

For sales above £6,000 but below £15,000 the amount of the gain which is taxed is restricted or limited. This is where it gets a little complex, because the gain is limited to an amount which is five thirds of the amount by which the sale proceeds exceed £6,000. For example, if I sold a painting for £9,000, then the maximum gain on which I could be taxed would be five thirds of the amount by which £9,000 exceeds £6,000. That is five thirds of £3,000. Five thirds is a strange fraction and, for those who are confused by mathematics, basically requires that the amount be multiplied by five and then divided by three. If we multiply £3,000 by five, that gives £15,000. If we then divide it by three we get £5,000; so the maximum gain I could be taxed on would be £5,000.

My actual gain would, of course, depend on how much I paid for the painting in the first place. If I paid £7,000 for it, then my actual gain would be £2,000 (remember that I sold it for £9,000) and the rule capping my maximum gain at £5,000 would have no effect. However, if I bought it for £1,000, then my actual gain would be £8,000 and the rule would apply; my gain would be capped at £5,000 and this is the amount on which I would then pay capital gains tax at either 18% or 28% depending on my income tax position.

Another issue that arises when it comes to selling chattels is the fact that they can sometimes be sold as part of a set. Think of a pair of antique vases for example, or a piece of antique furniture consisting of a table and four chairs. It is entirely possible that the set is worth more than the individual components. For example, each vase might alone be worth £2,000, but as a pair someone might well be willing to pay significantly more than £4,000 due to the fact that they are a matching pair, or set. In the case of a set, the £6,000 limit which we talked about above applies to the set and not to each item individually.

Thinking about the vases again, if I sell one vase for £2,000 it will be exempt from capital gains tax because the sale proceeds are below £6,000. If I sell the other vase to someone else for £2,000, then that will also be exempt because again it is less than £5,000. However, if I sell the pair as a set to one person for say, £10,000 then the sale will not be exempt because the proceeds for the set exceed £6,000. I cannot claim that this is two separate sales of £5,000 each and therefore that each is exempt from capital gains tax. This applies even where I break the set up and sell it off in parts; if I sell it to the same person (or same group of people acting together) then capital gains tax will potentially apply.

Finally for this chapter, it is important to be aware that the rules above can operate differently in relation to business assets, or chattels used within a business. In that case, and especially if those assets have attracted capital allowances, then even wasting assets can be subject to capital gains tax rules, so professional advice is needed. Those complex rules are beyond the scope of a book of this nature.

There are four main points that stem from this chapter. Firstly, disposals of chattels for no more than £6,000 do not generally attract capital gains tax. Secondly, wasting assets (those not expected to last more than 50 years) similarly do not generally attract capital gains tax. Thirdly, chattels which are not wasting assets but are sold for between £6,000 and £15,000 have a cap on the maximum gain that can arise. And finally, when dealing with a set of items, the set is treated as one asset, especially when it is sold to the same person.

Chapter 7 – Shares

One way of investing money into a company is to buy shares. By doing this I would become a shareholder and therefore the owner (or more likely, one of the owners) of the company. I could quite easily buy 500 shares in a high street bank or a supermarket. These companies have millions, if not billions, of shares and there is a readily accessible market in which I can buy their shares (called the stock exchange). If I buy 500 shares then I will own a very small part of that company. Often I will do this because I hope that the value of the shares will increase as the company grows, develops and improves its business and therefore its profits. In accordance with the advice given to any potential shareholder, the value of shares can go down as well as up. However, over the longer term (years rather than months) shares usually have a habit of increasing in value. Shares are therefore an asset on which I may have to pay capital gains tax on sale.

There is one feature of shares which makes the capital gains tax rules a little more complex. Most assets are easily identifiable. If I buy a painting, then obviously I can generally distinguish it from any other paintings I own. When it comes to selling the painting, it is clear which painting I am selling, and therefore working out how much I bought it for and the associated costs of the purchase is not a difficult task; when it comes to shares that might not be so easy. If I buy 500 shares in a supermarket, and then the following year I buy another 300, and then another 200 a couple of months later, then I will now have a holding of 1,000 shares. If I then decide to sell 400 shares two years later, the question arises as to which of the 1,000 shares I am selling. It is highly likely that the three separate purchases that I made were all made at different share prices, and those differing prices would affect the amount of the capital gain that I make on the sale. This issue gives rise to the special rules.

Let's work through an example to help illustrate the rules as we go along. Assume you buy 1,000 shares in ABC plc for £2 each and then a few months later you buy another 2,000 shares in the same company for £3 each. The following year you decide to sell 1,500 of your shares because they are now worth £5 each. If we use £2 as the cost of the shares, then your gain will be larger than if we used £3 as the cost. So what do we do?

Well first it is worth noting that there are special rules which apply if it turns out that you purchased shares in the same company on the same day as you disposed of the 1,500 shares. That is not the case here and it would be fairly unusual for the vast majority of people to do this. There is also a special rule that applies if it turns out that you purchased shares in the following 30 days after the sale. That again is not the case here and again it is not something which most people would do. If either of those special rules does apply, then the cost of those new shares is the cost which is initially used when calculating the gain on the sale, but specialist advice should certainly be sought.

Ignoring those rather unusual circumstances, shares in the same company which are bought at different times are "pooled" together into one holding. The costs of those shares are also pooled. On a sale of any of the shares, the proportion of shares sold is calculated and this proportion of the total costs can be used in the calculation. That all sounds a bit complicated so let's return to the example.

We said that the first thing you were going to do was to buy 1,000 shares in ABC plc for £2 each. That means that your "pool" of shares now consists of 1,000 shares and the total cost of those shares is £2,000. In the usual way, you can include any associated costs of actually buying the shares, such as stockbroker fees. Let's assume they were £200. Your cost "pool" is therefore £2,200.

We then said that a few months later you bought another 2,000 shares for £3 each (or £6,000 in total). You now own a total of 3,000 shares. The total cost of those shares is the £2,200 you spent on the first purchase plus the £6,000 you spent on the second purchase, plus any associated costs on the second purchase (let's assume these were £300). Your total cost pool is therefore now £2,200 plus £6,000 plus £300, which gives £8,500. So you now own 3,000 shares which cost, in total, £8,500.

You then decided to sell 1,500 of your shares the following year when the value of each share is £5. Remember, it is this disposal which would potentially give rise to the first capital gains tax charge in relation to your ownership of these shares.

The first step is to calculate the proportion of shares which you are now selling. As you are selling 1,500 shares out of the 3,000 that you own, I hope you can see that you are therefore selling exactly half, or 50% of your shareholding in ABC plc. You are selling them for £5 per share and so the total amount you will receive from the buyer is £5 multiplied by 1,500, which gives £7,500. When it comes to deducting the cost of these shares, you would simply apply the 50% proportion to the total cost of all your shares. We know that your total costs were £8,500, and so you can deduct 50% of this figure from your proceeds to work out your gain. 50% of £8,500 is £4,250. Your gain on the sale of the 1,500 shares will therefore be £7,500 minus £4,250, which gives £3,250.

From this you could deduct your costs incurred in the sale (these only relate to *this* sale and so are deductible in full). Assuming these costs were £100, then your gain is reduced to £3,150. As a reminder, if you made no further disposals for capital gains tax in the current tax year, then this gain would fall into your annual exemption (£11,100) and so no capital gains tax would be payable. If it is not covered by that exemption (because you had used it up on other gains for example) then you would pay capital gains tax at either 18% (if you are a basic rate taxpayer for income tax) or 28% (if you are a higher rate taxpayer).

A Really Basic Introduction to Capital Gains Tax

Following your sale of the 1,500 shares in ABC plc, your "pools" would be reduced as follows. The number of shares you own has dropped from 3,000 to 1,500 and so your "share pool" is adjusted accordingly. The total cost of your 3,000 shares was £8,500. Having used £4,250 of this cost in the sale of the 1,500 shares, the remaining "cost pool" is reduced from £8,500 to £4,250. Any further purchases of shares will be added to the pools and any further disposals will be deducted. Remember, each pool only applies to shares in the *same* company (and in fact only to the same *type* of shares in the same company). If I have shares in two or more different companies, then I would have a series of pools for each company.

There is one thing which we should note about shares before moving on. The above applies where someone buys and sells shares in a larger company which is probably listed on the stock exchange. This covers most shares that most people will buy and sell in their lifetime and includes shares in most companies which are household names. However, some people do own shares in smaller private companies and in that case professional advice should always be sought, because there are special reliefs which can be applied to share transactions in such companies.

We will look briefly at some of them later in the book, but others, such as the Enterprise Investment Scheme, are beyond the scope of this book.

This chapter has covered the capital gains tax issues involved in selling shares in large public companies. In particular, it has focused on the problem of identifying which shares have been sold when a shareholding might have been built up over a considerable period of time.

Chapter 8 – Tax reliefs

A tax relief is a good thing generally. It usually results in a person paying less tax than they would otherwise have done so without the relief. It is therefore important to take advantage of any tax reliefs whenever possible. This chapter will give a fairly brief overview of some of the main reliefs available.

We have in fact already looked at an important relief earlier in the book. We called this the private residence exemption and noted that it applied where a person sells their only or main private residence. We saw that it generally means that the vast majority of people will pay no capital gains tax on the sale of their house. Only if they have left it unoccupied, or have rented out parts of it or used it for business purposes for certain periods of time do they have to be concerned about capital gains tax. In those cases the rules are complex and expert advice should be sought.

Another fairly common situation to which a useful "relief" can be applied is the transfer of assets between spouses and civil partners. These transfers are generally not subject to capital gains tax in that no tax is payable when the transfer takes place. However, it is in effect more of a deferral rather than an exemption because the potential capital gains tax payable is actually "stored up" and becomes payable in full once the asset in question has been disposed of "outside" the marriage or partnership.

Let's look at an example. Edwina and Frances are civil partners. Edwina buys an antique vase for £1,000. She then gives it to Frances a couple of years later when the vase is worth £3,000. At this time there is no capital gains tax payable despite the increase in value. However, when Frances sells the vase ten years later for £15,000, her gain will be calculated using the original cost *to the civil partnership* of the vase. In other words, her basic gain would be £15,000 less the £1,000 that Edwina originally paid for it (less any incidental costs as usual and of course her annual exemption). So we see that in fact the civil partnership or married couple are treated as one "unit" for capital gains tax purposes. The people involved can transfer assets between them as many times as they wish, and capital gains tax will not become an issue until the asset is disposed of to someone outside that unit.

It is worth noting a couple of things here about gifts. Generally, a gift will attract capital gains tax in the same way that a sale would. Rather than using the sale proceeds as our starting point, we use the market value of the asset at the time of the gift. If I give away a painting worth £5,000, then I am treated as having sold it for £5,000. I can then deduct the amount that it cost me to buy originally, and any associated costs of purchase and sale in the usual way. Again, my annual exemption can also be used against the gain.

What is most relevant about gifts for this chapter is that gifts made to a charity are exempt from capital gains tax. There are some complex rules here, for example, it is essential that the asset has been gifted in its entirety and that you do not retain any kind of interest in it. This might be a problem if you gifted your house but continued to live in it for example.

Another relief that can apply to people in their personal capacity rather than in a business sense (which we will consider in a moment) is a relief that applies to employee share schemes. An employee share scheme is a scheme which employers run to incentivise or reward their employees. In fact there are different types of employee share scheme and the tax treatment of such schemes varies. The rules are complex and careful consideration needs to be given to the detail of each scheme. However, generally such schemes give rise to capital gains tax reliefs, sometimes up to a limit. They are usually more tax efficient than simply gifting shares to employees outright. Some schemes involve an option to buy shares. An option is where an employee has a choice to buy shares in the future at a price fixed today. Hopefully the shares go up in value in the intervening period, which means that the employee ends up buying shares for less than they are actually worth at the time of the purchase. Often, when the employee sells the shares, the cost which is used in the calculation is the value of the shares at the time of the exercise of the option rather than the actual price paid for the shares; this results in a smaller gain and therefore less tax than would otherwise be the case. As I say, such schemes are complex and the detail is certainly beyond the scope of an introductory book of this nature.

Capital gains tax relief can also be obtained on certain investments such as ISAs (or NISAs as they are now often called), again up to certain limits and certain types of bonds.

Other important capital gains tax reliefs apply in more of a business setting. These reliefs include entrepreneurs' relief, roll-over relief, hold over relief and incorporation relief.

Entrepreneurs' relief came into effect in April 2008. It applies to people who are in business or who own a certain percentage of a company which carries on a trade of some kind. Where such a person sells the business or part of it (including the assets after the business has ceased to trade) or where a person sells shares in a company in which they own at least 5% of the shares, then the relief may well apply. Note that the relief does not apply to companies as such, but to individuals who sell shares in companies.

The effect of entrepreneurs' relief is that the rate of capital gains tax that is payable is 10% rather than the usual rate of up to 28%. There is a limit on the amount of gain to which a person can apply entrepreneurs' relief in their lifetime, but that limit is currently set at £10 million and so for most people it will be more than enough to cover any such gains.

As ever, there are complicated rules about what constitutes a trade, so expert advice will be needed should this relief ever need to be applied in practice. It can, however, give rise to considerable tax savings and so obtaining the advice may well turn out to be worth any related cost.

Let's look at an example of entrepreneurs' relief in operation. Graham trades in partnership as an accountant. He originally invested £50,000 in order to buy his share in the partnership. He is now receiving £150,000 on the sale of his share due to his retirement. His gain is clearly £100,000 (we'll ignore the costs he incurred on the purchase and the sale of his partnership share to keep things simple). He can deduct his annual exemption of £11,100 from his gain. That leaves a gain of £88,900. Because he is selling his share in the business, he should qualify for entrepreneurs' relief and, assuming he has not used up all of his £10 million of lifetime gains, he will pay capital gains tax at 10%. The amount of tax will therefore be £8,890.

Let's move on to the next "business" relief, which is roll-over relief. Roll-over relief applies to businesses. A business includes people who work for themselves, people who trade in partnership with other people, and companies. The relief is aimed at businesses which replace certain assets with new ones. Those assets include, amongst other more specialised assets, land and buildings and fixed plant and machinery. Fixed plant and machinery usually involves large items annexed to land or buildings, such as cranes.

The relief itself is a little complex in its operation, but generally allows a business which is replacing assets to roll over any gain made on the sale of the old asset into the purchase of the new asset. The result is that capital gains tax is not paid when the old asset is sold, but when the new asset is sold. Let's consider an example.

Harriet decides that her business needs new premises and so she sells her shop for £150,000 incurring a gain of £40,000. Rather than having to pay capital gains tax on this gain in the usual way, she could roll the gain over into the new shop. Assuming she buys a new shop for more than £150,000, then she can roll the entire gain over into the new shop, leaving her no tax to pay now.

However, it will have an impact when she sells her new shop in the future. Let's assume the new shop cost £200,000. The cost of the new shop is reduced by the amount of the gain from the original sale. In this case the cost of the new shop will be reduced from £200,000 to £160,000. If we think about this for a moment, it is having the effect of *increasing* the gain on the sale of the new shop. If she sold it for £300,000, her gain would have been £100,000 (£300,000 minus £200,000). However, her actual gain will be £140,000 (£300,000 minus the revised cost of £160,000). In effect she will then be paying capital gains tax on *both* sales (although not quite).

So roll-over relief is another relief which is more of a deferral than a relief. Having said that, when Harriet sells her new shop in the future, if she reinvests the proceeds into a *third* shop, she will be able to roll-over the whole gain a second time. In this way, it may be many years before she has to pay any capital gains tax.

As ever there are complications with roll-over relief. The relief is restricted where the asset is not used entirely, or continuously for business purposes. It is also restricted when not all of the proceeds are reinvested into the new asset. There are other conditions too so again expert advice should be sought before claiming this relief.

However, there is one main condition that is worth looking at here, and that is in respect of timing. The new asset must be purchased within the three year period after the old asset is sold or within the period of one year before it is sold. For example, if Harriet above sold her shop on 1st March 2016, she would have until 1st March 2019 to reinvest the proceeds, or she would have needed to have already reinvested them since 1st March 2015. Note that it is not the *actual* proceeds that need to be invested, just a matching sum of money.

The next "business" relief to consider is hold-over relief. The name is such that students of tax often confuse it with roll-over relief. However, hold-over relief is quite different. Hold-over relief applies where a business asset is given away or sold for less than its full value. This relief applies to people who work for themselves or work in partnership with other people. It can also apply to people who effectively own at least 5% of the shares in a company if the asset is used by that company. In fact, it can also apply to the actual shares in such a company which can be treated as a business asset for the purposes of this relief.

The question that arises in relation to the practical application of this relief is this: why would the owner of a business want to give assets away? After all, business people are in business to make money and so gifting assets in this way would seem to go against this entrepreneurial principle. However, there is one situation in particular where businesses and business assets are sometimes gifted and that is between family members. It is not uncommon for parents to pass businesses down the line to their children for example. If a capital gains tax charge arose on such a gift, then it would seem a little unfair on the parents as they will have received no money from which to settle the tax bill. Hold-over relief provides a solution to this problem. It allows the potential capital gains tax charge to be "held-over" to the recipient of the business. In other words, no tax is payable when the gift is made, but it might well become payable when the business is eventually sold by the recipient. In that way, the tax is deferred rather than avoided. However, liability for the tax is transferred or held-over from one person (the person making the gift) to another (the recipient) and hence the name "hold-over" relief.

As you might expect, both parties to the transaction must agree to the relief taking effect, and this is done by signing a joint declaration for HM Revenue & Customs.

Let's consider an example of how this relief works. Ian owns his own business and has done for many years. He is now approaching an age at which he wants to take more of a "back seat" role in the business and on that basis he has decided to give the business his daughter Joanna. The business is worth around £200,000, and he bought it for £50,000 some years ago. The gain which arises when Ian gives the business to Joanna is £150,000 (the market value less the original cost). If both Ian and Joanna elect for hold-over relief to operate, then Ian will not pay any capital gains tax on the gift. The gain will be "held-over" to Joanna, who will face a larger capital gains tax bill than she otherwise would have done when she comes to sell the business in the future. The "cost" to her of the business will be the £200,000 it is worth at the date of the gift, less the amount of the gain which has been held-over (£150,000) which gives a cost of £50,000. If we assume that she eventually sells it for £500,000, then rather than her gain being £300,000 as it would have been (£500,000 minus £200,000), it will be £450,000 (£500,000 minus £50,000).

The position is complicated if, rather than gifting the business, Ian received less than the full value of the business from Joanna. This is often referred to as a partial gift and has the effect of restricting the amount of hold-over relief available. The detailed rules are beyond the scope of this book.

The final relief which we will cover here is called incorporation relief. This is a relief that applies when a business is incorporated. That means that a person who trades in business for themselves or with other people (in other words, as a sole trader or in a partnership) decides to operate through a company in future. A company is a formal organisation which must be created by undertaking certain legal steps and generally registering the company at Companies House. On the transfer of the business from the sole trader or partners to the company, there will usually be no capital gains tax to pay as long as the whole business is transferred as a going concern. The gain is then "rolled-over" into the shares of the company and the gain is realised or becomes subject to tax when those shares are eventually sold. Specialist advice should always be taken but, assuming the conditions are satisfied, the relief applies automatically and does not need to be applied for.

In this chapter we have considered some of the most common capital gains tax reliefs. We have seen that relief is often available on transfers of assets between spouses and civil partners, on transfers to charity, and in relation to employee share schemes. We have also looked at a range of "business asset" reliefs which apply when someone disposes of a business asset in certain situations.

Chapter 9 – Losses

As we have seen, capital gains tax is a tax payable when I sell certain assets for a profit. However, what happens if I sell one of those assets for a loss? The basic answer is quite straightforward. In any particular tax year I can set my losses off against my gains (we looked at tax years at the end of chapter 2; a tax year runs from 6th April in one year to the 5th April in the next). What this means is that I should work out the gain or loss that I have made on each asset that I sell. I should then add up all the gains and I can then deduct all the losses. The remaining balance is my total gain for the year. From this figure I can then deduct my annual exemption and only if there is anything left do I need to pay capital gains tax.

For example, Kamal sells a painting and makes a gain of £20,000. This would ordinarily be more than his annual exemption (£11,100) and therefore require him to pay some capital gains tax. However, Kamal has, in the same tax year, also sold a plot of land on which he made a loss of £9,000. At the end of the tax year, Kamal can deduct this loss from his gains to find his "net" position. It is clear from these figures that he will have made a net gain of £11,000. As this gain falls within his annual exemption, he will not have any capital gains tax to pay for the tax year. (Obviously, if his net gain had been above the annual exemption, then he would have to pay tax on that part of his net gain which was not covered by the exemption).

Losses which cannot be used in a particular year can be "carried forward" to later years and used against gains which arise in those later years. For example, if we assume that Kamal actually made a loss of £12,000 on his plot of land rather than £9,000, then he would not need to use all of that loss in the tax year in which it was created. Kamal made a gain of £20,000 in that year from the painting. All he needs to do to pay no capital gains tax is to use £8,900 of the loss made on the sale of the plot of land to reduce his gains to £11,100. At that point he will pay no capital gains tax because his gains now equal his annual exempt amount. The loss he made was £12,000 and he used £8,900 of it. He therefore has £3,100 of losses left and he can carry that forward to future tax years. If he then sells an asset in the next tax year for a gain of £30,000, he could use the £3,100 loss left from the previous tax year to reduce this gain to £26,900, thereby reducing the capital gains tax that he would have to pay in that next year. Unused losses can be carried forward in that way indefinitely and used whenever the need arises (in other words when the next capital gain arises).

The important thing to note about losses is that they arise in the same way and in the same circumstances as gains. In other words, losses made on assets which are generally exempt from capital gains tax cannot be used to reduce gains in this way. Losses on the sale of wasting assets (assets expected to last less than 50 years) cannot generally be used to reduce gains. Losses on the sale of assets for less than £6,000 are generally restricted to the loss that would have arisen had the asset been sold for £6,000.

The basic question is: would the asset have attracted capital gains tax if it had made a gain? If so, then any loss that is actually made is likely to be a loss which can be deducted from other gains in the same tax year.

There is a special rule for assets which you still own but which now have a negligible value. The detail is beyond the scope of this book but the rules mainly apply to shares which have lost their value. It is possible that the loss can be claimed against any gains made even though the shares have not been disposed of.

There are other special rules for the sale of shares in smaller companies which are not listed on the stock exchange but these are beyond the scope of this book. Specialist advice will certainly be needed when selling (or buying) those kinds of shares.

This chapter has considered the basic position in relation to capital losses. The general position is that they can only be set off against capital gains made in the same tax year, or carried forward and set off against capital gains made in future years.

Chapter 10 – Companies

So far this book has looked at capital gains tax primarily from the point of view of individuals, including individuals in business for themselves (sole traders) and in partnership with others (partnerships). In this final chapter I want highlight some of the main differences between these principles and the taxation of capital gains for companies.

A company is an organisation through which people can conduct business and other activities. It has an "artificial" legal personality and is therefore subject to taxation in its own right. The main tax which companies pay is called corporation tax. The first thing to note is that companies do not pay capital gains tax in the same way as individuals do. Instead, they pay corporation tax on any capital gain that they make. Such gains are called "chargeable gains".

The basic calculation of a capital gain is very similar to the one we have looked at for individuals. If a company buys a piece of land for £100,000 sells it for £250,000, then assuming the land was a capital asset (one used within the trade rather than one bought primarily to sell at a profit) then the basic gain that arises will be £150,000, just as it would be for an individual. The costs relating to the purchase and the sale can also be deducted in much the same way as they are for individuals (for example, legal costs). Any improvement expenditure which is reflected in the value of the land on sale can also be deducted, again, in much the same way as we saw for individuals. However, there are a couple of important differences which we should mention here for completeness.

Firstly, and most straightforwardly, companies do not get the benefit of an annual exemption. We saw that individuals can make gains of up to £11,100 in any one tax year before they need to start paying capital gains tax. Companies do not receive any such exemption.

Secondly, companies receive the benefit of something called indexation allowance. This is an allowance which tries to cancel out the effects of inflation. It is well known that money tends to lose its value over time (think about how much a loaf of bread cost ten years ago compared with today's prices). The fact is that generally things go up in price as money loses its value in this way. The tax that companies pay on their gains is aiming to tax the gain made *over and above* inflation. The rates at which indexation allowance is given can be found on the gov.uk website, linked from the capital gains tax part of the HM Revenue & Customs website. The rates are found in monthly tables which give the rate that applies to assets sold in that month. Each monthly table contains rates which vary according to when the asset was first purchased. I think it might be a good time for an example!

Loopy Limited purchased a piece of land in February 2004 for £100,000. It sold the land for £300,000 in September 2014. Looking at the tables on the gov.uk website, the rate applicable for an asset sold in September 2014, and purchased in February 2004 is 0.402. This is the figure by which the purchase price of the asset must be indexed. In other words we multiply the cost of £100,000 by 0.402 and add it to the £100,000. The result is an indexation allowance of £40,200, which gives an indexed purchase price of £140,200. What this is saying is that £100,000 in 2004 is worth £140,200 in 2014. Or to put it another way, if I had bought £100,000 of anything in 2004, it would be worth £140,200 in 2014 simply due to the effects of inflation. By using the revised purchase price of £140,200 in our calculation, we are cancelling out the effects of inflation, and just calculating the increase in value *above* inflation.

A Really Basic Introduction to Capital Gains Tax

The revised gain is therefore the £300,000 that Loopy Limited sold the land for, minus the revised purchase price of £140,200, giving a gain of £159,800. It is this figure on which the company will pay corporation tax at the current rates. Note that any expenditure related to the original purchase and any later improvement expenditure will also need to be indexed using the applicable rates from the tables.

Companies can also take advantage of some of the other reliefs we looked at earlier in the book. The main one is perhaps roll-over relief, applicable when a company replaces one of its assets. The gain is rolled-over into the purchase of the new asset in the same way as it is for individuals. There are some other reliefs which apply just to companies, but these are beyond the scope of an introductory book of this nature, not least because this book is about capital gains tax and, as I said above, companies do not pay capital gains tax, but corporation tax on their capital gains.

This chapter has considered very briefly the position relating to companies. As they pay corporation tax, further consideration is left to be covered by books on that topic.

Printed in Poland
by Amazon Fulfillment
Poland Sp. z o.o., Wrocław